Simple Technology

Slopes

written by Mandy Suhr
and illustrated by Mike Gordon

WAYLAND

First published in Great Britain in 1996
by Wayland (Publishers) Ltd
This edition printed in 2001 by Hodder Wayland

This revised edition published in 2009 by Wayland,
338 Euston Road, London NW1 3BH

Wayland Australia,
Level 17/207 Kent Street, Sydney, NSW 2000

Copyright © Wayland 1996

British Library Cataloguing in Publication Data
Suhr, Mandy.
    Slopes. -- (Simple technology)
    1. Inclined planes--Juvenile literature.
    I. Title II. Series
    621.8'11-dc22

ISBN 978-0-7502-5951-4

Printed in China

Wayland is a division of Hachette Children's Books,
an Hachette UK Company
www.hachette.co.uk

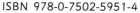

Contents

If you had to climb a mountain,
how would you do it?

Would you climb straight up a
steep mountainside?

Or take a longer route following
a gentle slope?

Both ways would take you
to the top of the mountain,
but which would take
less effort?

Slopes can make moving upwards a lot easier. The Egyptians built slopes to help them build the pyramids.

The stones were heavy and could
not be lifted from the ground.
It was a lot easier to move the
huge blocks of stone up a slope.

We use slopes in our homes to travel from one floor to another. Stairs are slopes made from steps.

Ramps are slopes. They can
be used to raise people...

...and vehicles from one level to another.

Coming down a slope can be fun!
A helter-skelter is a long slope
that goes around and around.

Some tools use slopes.

A screw has a long sloping
edge, called a thread, that
winds around in a spiral.
It's a bit like a helter-skelter!

Cut out a paper triangle.
The long side is the slope.

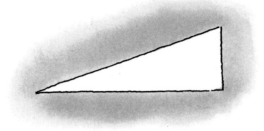

Wind it around a pencil. Can you see
how the slope winds around in a spiral
shape, like the thread on a screw?

Try pushing a nail into a piece of wood. It is not possible without a hammer.

But you can use a screwdriver to push a screw into a piece of wood.

When you turn the screw, the thread travels a long way. It goes around and around in the wood, and the screw moves in a little way. This takes much less effort than pushing something straight in.

You use screws all the time.
When you turn a tap you
are turning a hidden screw.
This opens and closes the
hole that lets water through.

A corkscrew is a tool for getting a tightly fitting cork out of a bottle.

A wedge is another useful type of slope. It is useful because its shape means it can be pushed between two surfaces.

A wooden wedge can be used to make something stop moving.

An axe is a metal wedge. Its shape makes splitting an object in half easy. When the thin end enters the object its shape pushes the two sides apart.

In the same way that slopes help you to move upwards easily, they can help you to travel downwards quickly, too.

Put a toy car on a flat surface.
Now raise one end of the surface.
What happens to the car?

Now try this experiment

You will need:
- building blocks
- a wooden plank
- a toy car
- a tape measure
- a piece of chalk

First, rest one end of the plank on one building block. Put the car at the top of the slope. Notice how fast the car travels. Then measure the distance that the car travelled.

Add more blocks and watch the car roll down the slope again. What do you notice about the speed of the car and the distance travelled as the slope is increased?

Make a penny drop game

You will need:
- balsa wood (1 cm and 0.5 cm thick)
- PVA glue
- a ruler
- a pencil
- a balsa wood knife
- ask an adult to help you

1. Ask a grown up to cut out a baseboard from the balsa wood 0.5 cm thick using the wood knife. Mark line across the board with a pencil.

8 cm
5½ cm
5½ cm
5½ cm
25 cm
30 cm

2. Ask an adult to cut out 4 triangles from balsa wood 1 cm thick.

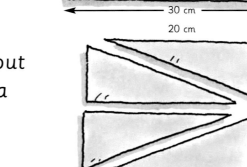

20 cm
5½ cm

3. Glue them on to the lines on the baseboard with the short edges butting up to the sides. Leave to dry.

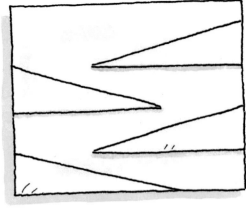

4. Cut out 4 more strips of balsa wood, 0.5 cm thick. Two should be 25 cm x 5 cm and the other two 30 cm x 5 cm.

5. Glue the strips around the edge of the baseboard to make a frame.

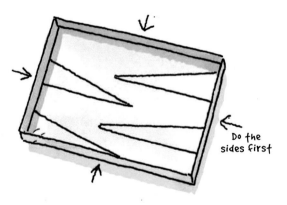

Do the sides first

Paint it brightly. Then tilt your penny drop game to make a penny run down the slopes.

27

Glossary

Effort
The force used to do work, e.g. lifting a heavy object.

Pyramid
A large triangular building which the ancient Egyptians built to hold the body of a dead king or queen.

Ramp
A slope used as a machine to make work easier.

Screw
A nail with a spiral groove around it so that it can be put in a hole and twisted. It is used to fasten things together.

Notes for adults

Simple Technology is a series of elementary books designed to introduce young children to the everyday machines that make our lives easier, and the basic principles behind them.

For millions of years people have been inventing and using machines to make work easier. These machines have been constantly modified and redesigned over the years to make them more sophisticated and more successful at their task. This is really what technology is all about. It is the process of applying knowledge to make work easier.

In these books, children are encouraged to explore the early inspirations for machines, and the process of modification that has brought them forward in their current state, and in doing so, come to an understanding of the design process.

The simple text and humorous illustrations give a clear explanation of how these machines actually work, and experiments and activities give suggestions for further practical exploration.

Suggestions for further activities

* Make a collection of slopes either in actual or picture form and discuss their uses. Include less obvious slopes such as screws, nuts and bolts.

* Investigate the principle of friction. Test out slopes with different surfaces and record and display your results.

* Explore the principle of gravity to encourage an understanding of why coming down a slope is easier than going up a slope.

* Visit a playground and go down a slide. How can the children slow down or speed up a journey? Roll a ball down a slide. Does this travel faster than a person?

Further information

Amazing Science: Forces and Motion by Sally Hewitt (Wayland, 2007)

Simple Machines: Wedges and Ramps by Chris Oxlade (Franklin Watts, 2007)

Little Bees: Push it, Pull it by Claire Llewellyn (Wayland, 2009)

Ways into Science: Push and Pull by Peter Riley (Franklin Watts, 2007)

Adult reference

The Way Things Work by David Macaulay and Neil Ardley (Dorling Kindersley, 2004)

Available as DVD (Dorling Kindersley, 2005)

Index